REDBACK
publishing

First published 2022 by
Redback Publishing
Australia

www.redbackpublishing.com.au
orders@redbackpublishing.com.au

ISBN 978-1-761400-32-2 PBK

Author: Peter Turner
Editor: Caroline Thomas
Designer: Redback Publishing

Original illustrations © Redback Publishing 2024
Originated by Redback Publishing

A catalogue record for this book is available from the National Library of Australia

Acknowledgements
Abbreviations: l—left, r—right, b—bottom, t—top, c—centre, m—middle
We would like to thank the following for permission to reproduce photographs: (Images © shutterstock)

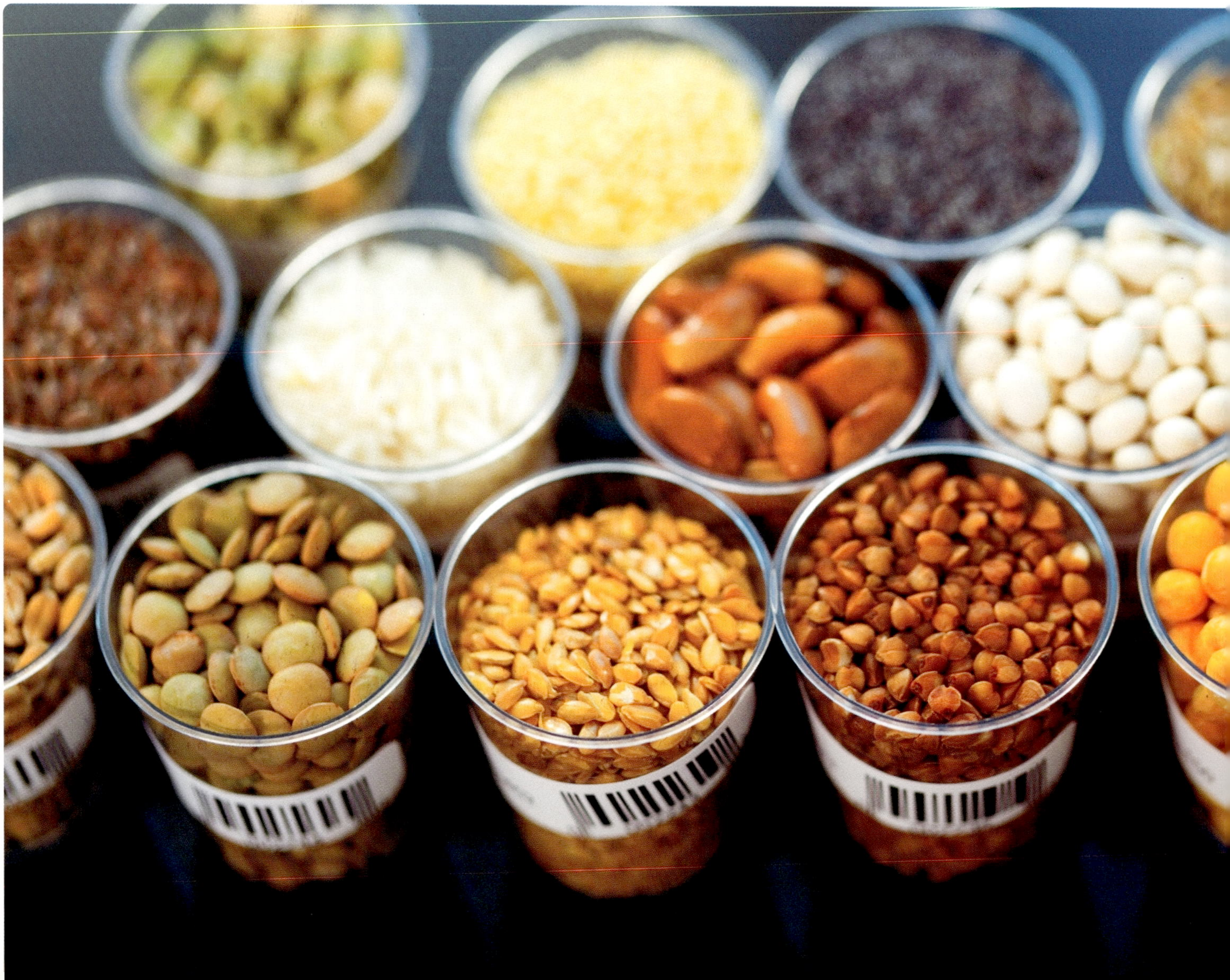

CONTENTS

WORKING IN THE FOOD INDUSTRY

The food industry in Australia is very important to the country's economy. Next time you eat something, think about where it came from, who produced it, how it was processed, and why it was packaged in a particular way.

Australia has a variety of climates and land types that allow farmers to produce a broad range of food. Farms range from small hobby farms to vast sheep and cattle stations. A job in food production might include, cattle, sheep, pig and poultry farming, dairy farming, or fruit, vegetable and grain growing.

WORK TYPES

Today, food production relies heavily on the latest scientific research and technologies and there are many opportunities for employment in agricultural and food science. At every stage of food production, from the farm to the plate, people are employed to provide the food that we all eat.

KEY AREAS IN FOOD PRODUCTION

- PREPARATION
- PROCESSING
- PACKAGING
- SALES AND MARKETING

PREPARATION

Food preparation involves preparing food for people to eat. The hospitality industry provides many jobs in this area, but lots of people are also employed in other areas including preparing meals for airlines, hospitals and nursing homes, and the pre-packaged meals industry.

PACKAGING

Food packaging has become very sophisticated and scientific. Packaging is designed and constructed for specific reasons, including food preservation, ease of transport and storage, **environmental impact**, and how attractive it is to customers. Designing and constructing packaging provides jobs for scientists, engineers, graphic designers, artists and copywriters.

PROCESSING

The processed food and beverage industry is Australia's largest manufacturing industry. It includes meat and dairy processing, fruit and vegetable processing, and bakery and confectionery manufacturing. Processing changes food from its natural state and often **preserves** it so that it remains edible for longer. Fruits, vegetables, meats, fish and dairy are all processed in different ways. Food processing has become **mechanised** and this provides many jobs in factories and processing plants alongside traditional methods.

SALES AND MARKETING

The business of selling food involves people trained in sales, advertising and marketing. Food is sold through **wholesale** and **retail** outlets including markets, specialist shops, supermarkets and milk bars. Marketing and advertising are important aspects of the food industry. Advertising creates public awareness and helps to stimulate demand.

DAIRY FARMING

Dairy farming involves maintaining the farm, caring for livestock and milking the animals. There are over five thousand dairy farms in eight unique regions across Australia. Dairy farms produce milk, yogurt and cheese and can offer a variety of job opportunities.

DAIRY FARMER

JOB DESCRIPTION

Dairy farmers look after the farm and manage the milking. They need practical, organisational and business skills.

RANGE OF WORK:

- manage the farm as a business
- maintain the condition of the land
- maintain fencing, equipment and farm vehicles
- plan and manage the feeding and protection of the dairy herd
- manage the milking
- look after the health of the herd
- organise breeding programs
- manage the **calving** and rearing of calves

EDUCATION AND TRAINING

Dairy farming is a specialised business. Many family-operated dairy farms pass on skills to their children. Working with a farmer or studying dairy and rural business management at a university, **TAFE** or agricultural college will also provide the necessary skills.

DAIRY FARM WORKER

JOB DESCRIPTION

Dairy farm workers help farmers with feeding, raising calves and milking livestock. They need good all round practical skills and should be skilled and confident when handling livestock. Dairy farm workers perform a wide range of general farming tasks. They also have duties that are specific to working on a dairy farm.

RANGE OF WORK:

- move the cows from the paddocks to the milking sheds
- prepare the cows for milking
- attach milking equipment and supervise the milking
- wash and sterilise milking machines
- clean the yards after milking

EDUCATION AND TRAINING

Dairy farm workers do not need any specific qualifications, although it helps to have general agricultural experience. Many dairy farm workers complete a certificate in agriculture and dairy production while working on a dairy farm.

MILK TANKER DRIVER

JOB DESCRIPTION

Milk tanker drivers transfer milk from a cooling tank on a farm into a tanker. It is then transported to a dairy processing plant where it is processed for packaging. Tanker drivers interact with farmers, farm workers and dairy staff. They need good communication skills, must be reliable and responsible and be able to cope with all driving conditions.

RANGE OF WORK:

- collect milk according to delivery instructions
- calculate load weight limits
- drive the tanker to its destination
- transfer the milk into and out of the tanker
- perform routine checks on brakes, tyres, oil and electrical systems

EDUCATION AND TRAINING

Milk tanker drivers need a special truck licence. Some drivers complete an apprenticeship in transport and distribution.

MILKING MACHINE TECHNICIAN

JOB DESCRIPTION

Milking machine technicians install and maintain the machines used for milking. They need to enjoy manual work and have good mechanical skills. Milking machine technicians also need good communication skills.

EDUCATION AND TRAINING

Milking machine technicians need a TAFE certificate or diploma in electrical engineering or plumbing. There are also apprenticeships in **milk harvesting**.

MY STORY

My father and my grandfather were dairy farmers and I can't imagine doing anything else. The work changes all the time. It's probably hardest during the calving season when you might be up all night, then have to work the next day. The hours are long, but there is some flexibility, especially in autumn when there is no calving. I like living and working in the same place so I can see the family during the day.

A few words of advice:
Dairy farming is difficult and expensive to get into so get an education to make sure you really know what you're doing. Try to get an ***apprenticeship****.*

PETER FITZGERALD
DAIRY FARMER

'Try to get an apprenticeship.'

MEAT PRODUCTION

Australia is recognised in many countries around the world as a supplier of high-quality meat. Apart from lamb, beef, pork and chicken there is also a growing demand for kangaroo, venison and emu meat. The industry provides many jobs in production, processing, packaging and meat or cattle transportation.

STATION MANAGER

JOB DESCRIPTION

Stations are large scale farms which usually rear either sheep or cows. The land is often leased from state or territory governments.

RANGE OF WORK:

- manage the station finances
- hire and supervise staff
- buy and sell stock
- supervise the maintenance of station property and equipment
- supervise branding, immunising, shearing, **crutching** and **dipping**
- prepare stock for slaughter
- control pests and weeds

EDUCATION AND TRAINING

Up-to-date information and skills are essential to the role of a station manager. Some station managers learn their skills from experienced farmers but many have formal qualifications. Previous management experience and/or qualifications are an advantage, while others progress within stations. There are diplomas and degrees in agriculture or animal science, with specialisations in rural management.

MEAT INSPECTOR

JOB DESCRIPTION

Meat inspectors make sure that meat and meat products are safe to eat.

RANGE OF WORK:

- check animals before and after slaughter
- check the quality and safety of meat
- identify disease and other problems in meat and meat products
- collect and send samples of blood, fat and tissue to be tested
- supervise disposal of meat not passed as fit for human consumption
- make reports and give evidence in court

EDUCATION AND TRAINING

Meat inspectors complete an apprenticeship in meat processing or study for a TAFE certificate in meat processing, concentrating on meat safety. Experience working in a meat processing environment is also generally required.

JACKEROO/ JILLAROO

JOB DESCRIPTION

Men performing this job are called jackeroos and women performing this job are called jillaroos. The job involves a range of work on sheep and cattle stations in return for accommodation and wages. This is an introductory position for people to gain experience and to progress further. Jackeroos and jillaroos must be physically fit, enjoy practical work and be comfortable working with animals.

RANGE OF WORK:

- look after livestock
- help **muster** sheep or cattle
- maintain vehicles and other farm equipment
- repair buildings and fences
- help with work such as haymaking
- perform administrative tasks

EDUCATION AND TRAINING

Working as a jackeroo or jillaroo does not require any formal education, and employers often provide on-the-job training. There are TAFE certificates which cover the practical aspects of introductory farm work. Traineeships in agriculture can specialise in sheep and wool or beef cattle production. Horse and/or motorbike riding skills can also improve work opportunities.

MEAT PROCESSOR

JOB DESCRIPTION

Meat processors handle the slaughtering, skinning and processing of livestock. They work with knives and saws so must have good hand-eye coordination, be responsible and be able to work efficiently. They must also meet strict hygiene and food handling standards.

EDUCATION AND TRAINING

There are no formal educational requirements for this job. Some workers receive on-the-job training, but it is also possible to do an apprenticeship in meat processing.

MY STORY

I come from a dairy-farming family, but I wanted to do something different. After I finished studying for a bachelor of agriculture I went into partnership with a friend who had some land. We borrowed some money from the bank and went into business. We put a lot of thought into writing a strong business plan as we knew we wanted to keep pigs outdoors rather than confined in sheds. It will take a while to build the business up and it's hard work. I like pigs - they're actually more responsive than people think.

A few words of advice:
If you want to go into farming, make sure you have an idea of what you're getting into. Try to get a job on a farm first - it will give you an idea of what's involved.

PATRICIA NIELSON
PIG FARMER

'Try to get a job on a farm first.'

GRAINS, FRUITS AND VEGETABLES

Australia's varied climate allows for a range of fruits and vegetables to be produced, from tropical sugar cane, bananas and mangoes in the north, to apples and soft fruit crops in the cooler south. Farmers, orchardists, market gardeners and berry growers plant, cultivate and harvest grains, vegetables, fruits and nuts.

CROP FARMER

JOB DESCRIPTION

Crop farmers manage farms that produce cereals, **pulses**, fruits or vegetables and grasses. They need to be motivated, practical and responsible. They must also be physically fit and good at problem solving.

RANGE OF WORK:

- plant, cultivate and harvest crops
- understand soil and climate conditions
- purchase farm equipment
- fertilise and **irrigate** crops
- arrange the sale of crops
- manage the farm's administration
- manage environmental effects on the crop

EDUCATION AND TRAINING

Specialised knowledge and experience is essential for working with certain crop types. Crop farmers can enrol in courses ranging from certificates to degrees through TAFE colleges and universities. Different courses deal with various areas of agriculture from animal science to crop growing and **horticulture**.

GRAIN AND SEED AGENT

JOB DESCRIPTION

Grain and seed agents sell grains, seeds, farming supplies and crops to farmers. They offer advice and solutions to problems that farmers might have regarding their crops. They need to be patient and attentive listeners and have strong communication skills.

RANGE OF WORK:

- blend mixtures of seeds
- supply farms with seeds, grains and fertilisers
- advise on various crops, soil conditions and methods of planting and harvesting
- advise on weed and pest control and the right fertilisers to use
- buy and sell harvested crops

EDUCATION AND TRAINING

There are no specific educational requirements to work as a grain and seed agent, although a degree or diploma in agriculture, horticulture or farm management will greatly enhance employment opportunities.

FRUIT AND VEGETABLE PICKER

JOB DESCRIPTION

Fruit and vegetable pickers harvest vegetables, fruits and nuts. Some picking is mechanised but most is done by hand. The work is seasonal and many pickers move around to find work. Pickers need to enjoy working outside, be able to cope with repetitive work and be fit enough to work quickly.

RANGE OF WORK:

- select and pick fruits and vegetables
- discard rotting fruits or vegetables
- operate harvesting machinery
- pack produce into cartons
- load produce onto trucks

EDUCATION AND TRAINING

There are no educational requirements for this job and most training takes place on-the-job.

AGRICULTURAL PILOT

JOB DESCRIPTION

Agricultural pilots fly aircraft and apply chemicals or fertilisers to farming land. They need good concentration and an ability to communicate well with people.

RANGE OF WORK:

- talk to the farmer about their requirements
- examine the area to be sprayed
- work out the amount of chemicals or fertilisers to be used
- understand weather patterns
- fly the aircraft to spray the crops

EDUCATION AND TRAINING

Pilots must complete both practical and theoretical training to obtain their licences. This training is available through flight training schools or at certificate, diploma and degree levels through TAFE colleges and universities.

MY STORY

I used to work for a manufacturing company but when they closed I was out of a job. I saw an advertisement for raspberry pickers and haven't looked back. I've picked cherries, plums, apples, strawberries, grapes and even cucumbers. I've been doing it for a few years now so I have places I go to regularly. I like getting to meet people of different ages and nationalities while I travel around Australia following the harvest. Plus the exercise keeps me fit. The only things I don't like are picking in the rain, getting to a place when the crop isn't ready, or there being too many pickers for the work.

A few words of advice:
Get some qualifications so you have choices about what you can do.

LES VAN RIET
FRUIT AND VEGETABLE PICKER

'Get some qualifications so you have choices.'

FISH AND SEAFOOD

Seafood is Australia's fourth most valuable food-based primary industry. It provides jobs in a combination of wild capture opportunities and aquaculture farming.

FISHERY OFFICER

JOB DESCRIPTION

Fishery officers are responsible for the protection and management of state and territory fishery resources. They must have excellent communication and negotiation skills and be prepared to work irregular hours.

RANGE OF WORK:

- patrol waterways
- inspect fishing boats and enforce fishing **quotas**
- enforce laws and investigate people who break them
- check that fish being sold are the correct sizes (not too young)
- advise on fishing regulations
- advise on marine management

EDUCATION AND TRAINING

Traineeships in the seafood industry are available through some TAFE colleges, and the Department of Primary Industries provides training courses. Tertiary qualifications in applied science are also useful.

FISH FARMER

JOB DESCRIPTION

Fish farmers raise fish or shellfish for sale. Anyone going into fish farming should be physically fit and have good business and communication skills. They should be happy working by themselves sometimes, as well as being part of a team.

RANGE OF WORK:

- breed fish from eggs or buy young fish
- transport fish and other aquatic stock to new tanks or beds
- maintain water quality
- prevent and treat disease
- manage administrative and financial matters
- maintain buildings and equipment
- kill, gut and pack fish

EDUCATION AND TRAINING

There are no formal educational requirements, but many fish farmers have a certificate or a diploma in aquaculture.

FISHING BOAT SKIPPER

JOB DESCRIPTION

Fishing boat skippers supervise the crew and organise daily operations on the boat. Working conditions can be unpredictable, so they need to be responsible, reliable and able to work well under pressure.

RANGE OF WORK:

- hire and supervise the crew
- plan work around weather patterns
- locate fishing areas
- navigate boats
- write reports
- supervise the equipping of the boat

EDUCATION AND TRAINING

Fishing boat skippers who are also master fishermen hold a skipper's licence. Conditions for this qualification vary from state to state, but involve spending time on a boat as well as classroom learning.

DECKHAND

JOB DESCRIPTION

Deckhands fish using nets, lines and pots. Senior deckhands can be responsible for small fishing boats or provide support to the skippers of large boats. Deckhands need to be physically fit, self-disciplined and able to work as part of a team. An understanding of boats and boat engines is also important.

RANGE OF WORK:

- help to operate fishing vessels
- load and unload fishing equipment
- cast out and haul in nets, lines and pots
- clean and process fish
- maintain and repair equipment

EDUCATION AND TRAINING

Inexperienced deckhands receive on-the-job training. Some TAFE colleges offer short courses in seafood industry studies or **traineeships** in the seafood industry (**aquaculture**).

MY STORY

I left school at 15 and worked lots of different jobs. Then one day I went abalone fishing with some mates and enjoyed it. I bought myself some diving equipment, put a down payment on a boat and learned to dive. You go out to where you think there will be plenty of abalone, dive off the boat and prise the abalone off the rocks with a knife.

To fish for abalone, it's important to understand the ocean and the weather. When the weather is good and the sea is calm it's one of the best jobs in the world, but diving can be very dangerous.

A few words of advice:
Join a diving club and get some experience, then work as a deckhand to find out whether you like it or not.

IAN MCKECHNIE
ABALONE FISHERMAN

'Join a diving club and get some experience ...'

GRAPES AND WINE

Winemaking is one of Australia's most important industries. New vineyards are being planted all the time, creating opportunities for employment in the wine industry as well as in retail, tourism and hospitality. Australian wines are also exported and highly regarded overseas.

VITICULTURIST

JOB DESCRIPTION

Viticulturists grow grapes for making wine. They coordinate the activities of workers who plant, cultivate and harvest grapes. Some viticulturists make their own wine and others sell their grapes to winemakers. People working in this area must be physically fit and have good organisational, business and management skills.

RANGE OF WORK:

- prepare soil for planting vines
- build trellises for supporting vines
- plant and cultivate vines
- monitor and manage pests and weeds
- control irrigation of vines
- prune vines and pick grapes
- manage administration and finance

EDUCATION AND TRAINING

Although some of the necessary skills can be learned by working with an experienced grape grower, most viticulturists have studied science, horticulture or viticulture at diploma or degree level.

WINERY WORKER

JOB DESCRIPTION

Winery workers support winemakers and are involved with all aspects of the winery. They must be physically fit and able to follow instructions.

RANGE OF WORK:

- help with grape planting, tending and harvesting
- operate winemaking equipment
- assist fermentation by turning or topping-up bottles
- assist with the bottling process
- help with wine tasting and cellar sales

EDUCATION AND TRAINING

There are no educational requirements for becoming a winery worker. On-the-job training is often given to workers or they can complete a TAFE certificate in food processing or the wine industry.

WINEMAKER

JOB DESCRIPTION

Winemakers coordinate and supervise all activities to do with winemaking. Some winemakers are responsible for grape growing as well as wine production. Winemakers need an excellent sense of taste and good communication skills.

RANGE OF WORK:

- deal with growers who provide grapes
- test grapes for ripeness, sweetness and acidity
- organise grape picking at the optimum time
- coordinate the testing and crushing of grapes, the **fermentation, fortifying, clarifying** and ageing of grapes and the cooling, filtering, and bottling processes
- monitor wine quality
- enter wines in shows and competitions
- organise tasting and tours of the winery

EDUCATION AND TRAINING

Winemakers usually study for a degree in applied science (wine or viticulture). An apprenticeship with an experienced winemaker would also be beneficial.

WINE SELLER

JOB DESCRIPTION

Wine sellers are responsible for the selection and sale of wine through wholesale and retail outlets. They need good customer service, organisational, business and communication skills.

RANGE OF WORK:

- arrange stock and place orders
- assist customers
- find new wines
- arrange deliveries

EDUCATION AND TRAINING

To work as a wine seller you need experience in sales and an understanding of the wine business. Retail training is usually provided on-the-job although it is possible to complete a qualification in retail operations through a TAFE college.

MY STORY

'Never waste an opportunity...'

*After I left school, I started washing dishes in a hospital, which led to an apprenticeship as a chef. Since then I've worked in almost every area of the hospitality industry, travelled extensively, run my own restaurant and worked in a winery. I was lucky to work for someone who showed me the importance of taking opportunities and I've been following that advice ever since. I've also gained qualifications in **viticulture**, business management and marketing. Now I help wineries by showing them how to market themselves effectively.*

A few words of advice:
Never waste an opportunity and learn from everything you do. Keep studying because diversity is the key to success.

DARREN MURPHY
MARKETING CONSULTANT

EGGS, CHEESE, HONEY AND OIL

Some animal products such as eggs, cheese, milk and honey can be obtained without harming the animal. Obtaining these animal products often requires special equipment or skills.

POULTRY FARMER

JOB DESCRIPTION

Some poultry farmers farm chickens for their meat while others keep hens to produce eggs. Poultry farmers need strong planning, organisational and marketing skills, as well as practical farming skills.

RANGE OF WORK:

- manage the feeding, care and health of hens
- ensure sheds and cages are clean
- collect, clean and grade eggs
- check and maintain equipment
- manage administration and finances
- market products

EDUCATION AND TRAINING

There are no specific educational requirements for this job, but many poultry farmers have a certificate or diploma in agriculture or farm management. Others have degrees in agricultural science.

APIARIST

JOB DESCRIPTION

Apiarists raise bees to produce honey, **royal jelly**, pollen and wax. Apiarists need to be prepared to work alone but must also communicate effectively with customers and suppliers. It helps to have carpentry and mechanical skills to be able to maintain the bee hives.

RANGE OF WORK:

- assemble and repair beehives
- monitor safety equipment
- control disease, **vermin** and **parasites**
- breed queen bees
- force bees from hives to inspect the hives and **harvest** the honeycomb
- collect royal jelly
- process beeswax
- rent hives to orchards and farms for pollination

EDUCATION AND TRAINING

Apiarists do not need formal qualifications, but there are important skills to learn and working with experienced beekeepers can provide these necessary skills. Some TAFE colleges offer short courses in beekeeping. Anyone keeping bees needs to register with the relevant state authorities.

OLIVE OIL PROCESSOR

JOB DESCRIPTION

The olive oil industry is a growing industry and employs an increasing number of people each year. Olive oil processors use an olive press to separate the vegetable fibres and fluids from the oil.

RANGE OF WORK:

- weigh, wash and de-leaf olives
- test olives for water content
- operate olive processing machinery
- monitor the oil settling in vats
- bottle the oil
- clean and maintain the machinery

EDUCATION AND TRAINING

Working as an oil processor does not require any formal qualifications although a certificate or diploma in agriculture or horticulture would be an advantage.

CHEESEMAKER

JOB DESCRIPTION

Cheesemakers use milk and other ingredients to make cheese. This can be a highly mechanised process, but some small companies still make cheese using traditional methods. Cheesemakers should be able to work as part of a team and must enjoy manual work.

RANGE OF WORK:

- heat milk to specific temperatures
- test milk for acidity
- mix and cook ingredients for different cheeses
- mix **rennet** into milk
- separate curds and whey
- monitor the production process
- take and test samples of cheese
- clean and sterilise equipment

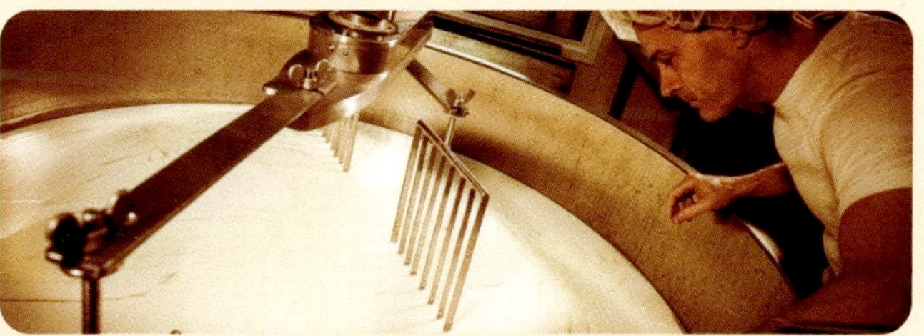

EDUCATION AND TRAINING

There are no formal educational requirements for becoming a cheesemaker. However, many cheesemakers complete a TAFE certificate, specialising in dairy processing.

MY STORY

After I left school I did a bachelor of applied science, specialising in horticulture. I'd been working with stone fruit and organic fruit and vegetables when I saw an advertisement for managing an olive oil processing company and thought it looked a bit different. I like this job because we do everything here - grow the trees, harvest the fruit, bottle the oil and market the product.

A few words of advice:
Get some qualifications in the general area that you're interested in. When you start working you get an idea of what's around, then you can start specialising.

DALE STEFFOX
MANAGER (OIL PROCESSING)

'get an idea of what's around, then start specialising.'

PROCESSING AND PRESERVING FOOD

Processing changes food from its natural state and preserves it so that it remains edible for longer. Fruits, vegetables, meats, fish and dairy foods are processed in a variety of ways including canning, freezing, bottling, dehydrating and smoking. Process workers must have good concentration and observation skills and be able to act quickly.

SMALLGOODS MAKER

JOB DESCRIPTION

Smallgoods makers prepare meat and operate meat-processing machinery to make meat products including sausages, hams and salami.

RANGE OF WORK:

- prepare meat by removing bones and fat
- operate, maintain and clean mincers, grinders and mixing machines
- grind, season and flavour meat
- shape the meat depending on the product
- **cure** and cook meat products
- operate, maintain and clean cooking kettles and smoking chambers

EDUCATION AND TRAINING

Smallgoods makers are usually required to complete an apprenticeship in meat processing through a TAFE college. This means finding an employer who will supervise the practical training. Experience working as a butcher is also advantageous.

DRYING MACHINE OPERATOR

JOB DESCRIPTION

Some foods are processed in ovens, kilns or vacuum drying equipment. Meats, fish, fruits, vegetables and coffee beans can be preserved by smoking and drying.

RANGE OF WORK:

- weigh and measure products
- test the moisture content of products
- set temperature and time controls
- feed products into machines
- check for spills and blockages

EDUCATION AND TRAINING

Many TAFE colleges offer traineeships in food processing, and employers also offer on-the-job training.

FREEZER TUNNEL OPERATOR

JOB DESCRIPTION

Freezer tunnel operators look after the machinery that freezes food products. Foods are frozen quickly to lock in freshness and nutrition.

RANGE OF WORK:

- operate the conveyor belt that transports food through the freezer
- control the speed of the conveyor belt
- monitor and adjust the freezer temperature
- remove excess ice and frost from the conveyor

EDUCATION AND TRAINING

There are no specific educational requirements for working as a freezer tunnel operator. TAFE colleges offer certificates in food processing, but many employees receive on-the-job training.

AT-SEA SEAFOOD PROCESSOR

JOB DESCRIPTION

Some deep-sea trawlers have factories on board. At-sea seafood processors work in these factories preparing and processing seafood products. They are at sea for long periods of time and must be physically fit, coordinated and safety conscious.

RANGE OF WORK:

- sort fish by size and species
- scrape scales from fish
- fillet and trim fish to size
- put fish into packs
- weigh and count packs
- sort frozen packs into cartons
- operate, maintain and clean machinery

EDUCATION AND TRAINING

There are no specific educational requirements for this job, but some at-sea seafood processors complete a certificate in seafood processing. Training in all aspects of the job including food handling and safety standards are provided on-the-job.

MY STORY

When I was home with young children I started looking for a way to earn money from home. I'd always liked bottling and preserving and made my own tomato sauce and bottled plums and cherries when they were in season. I thought I'd make more, do the bottles up nicely and see if anyone would buy them. Now I supply the local shops and some of the tourist spots like wineries and nurseries that have gift shops and cafes. I've got a friend helping me and we've expanded the range with chutneys and jams. Soon I have to rent premises as the business is really expanding.

A few words of advice:
Pay attention to your skills and interests as you never know when an opportunity might arise.

LEANNE SIM
SMALLGOODS MAKER

'Pay attention to your skills and interests ...'

BREADS, CAKES AND SWEETS

Bakers, pastry chefs and cake decorators work in specialist cake or bread shops, bakeries and factories. In factories and large bakeries the process can be highly mechanised but many workers still use traditional methods. Bakery workers need to be practical, creative, physically fit and able to work as part of a team. Most jobs in this area begin very early in the morning.

• BAKER

JOB DESCRIPTION

Bakers prepare and bake bread, pastries and cakes. Bakers often work very early in the morning or late at night.

RANGE OF WORK:

- measure and mix ingredients for doughs
- roll or mould dough into loaves and shapes
- monitor pans of dough as they rise
- regulate oven temperatures
- prepare orders and serve customers
- deliver goods
- inspect, maintain and clean equipment

EDUCATION AND TRAINING

Becoming a baker usually involves completing a traineeship through a recognised training body such as a TAFE college, then finding a job where someone is qualified to supervise training.

• PASTRY CHEF

JOB DESCRIPTION

Pastry chefs make cakes and pastries. They work in hotels, restaurants and cake shops, and some specialise as **pâtissiers** or **chocolatiers**.

RANGE OF WORK:

- make various kinds of pastry
- create and make a wide range of cakes and sweet breads
- make glazes and icing to decorate cakes and pastries
- follow all food health and safety regulations

EDUCATION AND TRAINING

Anyone wanting to work as a pastry chef should consider completing a TAFE apprenticeship or certificate in food processing, patisserie or similar.

CONFECTIONER

JOB DESCRIPTION

Confectioners make sweets, chocolates, toffees and boiled lollies. In factories much of the work is mechanised.

RANGE OF WORK:

- weigh, measure and heat ingredients
- control the temperature of boiling confectionery
- mix or knead ingredients
- coat confectionery with chocolate
- check batches of confectionery for quality
- sort, inspect and pack confectionery
- clean equipment and machinery

EDUCATION AND TRAINING

Skills for this job can be learned while working with an experienced confectioner, but many confectioners complete an apprenticeship. This means they get on-the-job training and qualifications through a TAFE college.

CAKE DECORATOR

JOB DESCRIPTION

Cake decorators use icing and **ganaches** to decorate cakes. They need patience, fine motor skills and a good sense of design.

RANGE OF WORK:

- shape cakes to client's design specifications
- colour and mix icing and ganache
- apply icing and ganache layers to build cakes
- pipe icing and ganaches to create artistic cake designs
- sculpt edible flowers, figures and other decorations
- adhere to all food safety standards

EDUCATION AND TRAINING

If cake decorators work with a baker or pastry chef, they might receive on-the-job training. Otherwise, TAFE colleges sometimes offer short courses in cake decorating.

MY STORY

When I left school I studied art, but I hated parting with my artwork so I was never going to make a living as an artist. I got a job at a bakers and found I really enjoyed the creative aspect of baking. I did an apprenticeship because I wanted to learn the skills properly. The job means working from 2.30 am to 10.30 am, which is when everyone else is asleep. I like this job because I'm a night owl naturally.

'working hours can affect the friends you see ...'

A few words of advice:
Make sure you understand how much these working hours can affects the friends you see, the places you go and the sports you play.

ADAM PARNCUTT
BAKER

PACKAGING, MARKETING AND ADVERTISING

Once food has been produced and processed, it is packaged and sold. Appropriate packaging must be designed before marketing and advertising can begin.

ADVERTISING COPYWRITER

JOB DESCRIPTION

Advertisements for foods appear in magazines, brochures, on television, radio and websites. Advertising copywriters write the words that go with these images and advertisements. Copywriters need to be creative and organised. They must be able to work to a deadline and understand the people they are writing for.

RANGE OF WORK:

- talk to the client about their needs
- research the product
- develop ideas and present them to the client
- draft the copy
- work with other members of a creative team

EDUCATION AND TRAINING

People can work as copywriters without formal qualifications but competition for jobs is high. It helps to have a diploma or a degree in professional writing, advertising, marketing, journalism or media studies.

PACKAGING TECHNOLOGIST

JOB DESCRIPTION

A food's packaging needs to keep its contents protected from contaminants such as dirt and moisture. It should help to keep the food fresh and make it easy to transport. Packing technologists design packaging. They need to be scientifically and mathematically minded, practical, creative and good at problem solving.

RANGE OF WORK:

- consider the cost of production
- design packaging
- solve packaging problems
- consider the impact of packaging on the environment
- test packaging under a range of conditions

EDUCATION AND TRAINING

Tertiary qualifications in packaging engineering or food technology are generally required. A university education in maths or science may also be accepted along with experience in the industry.

GRAPHIC DESIGNER

JOB DESCRIPTION

Graphic designers combine words and pictures to design art layouts for packaging, labels, brochures and other forms of advertising. Graphic designers need to be imaginative, creative and good at problem solving. They must be able to communicate with a range of people, manage their time and work to deadlines.

RANGE OF WORK:

- talk with clients to understand the brief
- prepare rough design sketches
- prepare layouts using photography, illustration and text
- work with feedback from clients
- present samples of finished layouts
- discuss production materials and cost

EDUCATION AND TRAINING

To work as a graphic designer you need a diploma or advanced diploma in graphic design. Many universities offer a bachelor of arts (graphic design) or a bachelor of visual arts.

MARKETING MANAGER

JOB DESCRIPTION

Marketing managers plan and direct the development and presentation of a company's products. They might also manage a company's public relations. Working in this area requires good research and communication skills and a clear understanding of the way people think and behave.

RANGE OF WORK:

- identify and respond to opportunities and threats in the marketplace
- investigate competing products
- prepare marketing plans
- identify who will buy the product
- plan advertising campaigns
- monitor marketing campaigns

EDUCATION AND TRAINING

There are no formal educational requirements for working in marketing but people usually have a diploma or degree in marketing, communications or another related field.

MY STORY

After I left school I did a degree in marketing and went to work with a big marketing company for a few years. I decided to go ***freelance*** *so that I could choose my clients and the kind of work I do. I usually work with companies who are having trouble letting people know who they are. I work with the client to improve public awareness of their brand and position in the marketplace. This can be done in all kinds of ways from creating a presence on the web, a social media advertising campaign or a combination of print and digital media. I can't say I like tight deadlines but I know that I work well under pressure.*

A few words of advice:
Get qualified and start looking for a job as soon as you start your studies.

MAGGIE CHEN
FREELANCE MARKETING CONSULTANT

'start looking for a job as soon as you start your studies.'

SELLING FOOD

In Australia, food is sold through a range of wholesale and retail outlets. These outlets include supermarkets, grocery stores, market stalls and specialist food shops.

SPECIALIST FOOD WORKER

JOB DESCRIPTION

Sometimes shops sell particular kinds of food. In these shops, the staff have specialised knowledge and training.

RANGE OF WORK:

- Fishmongers clean, gut and prepare fish and seafood ready for sale. Fishmongers recommend what is fresh and available and give advice on preparation and cooking.
- Butchers sell meat, poultry and meat products to the public. Butchers cut, bone and trim meat, serve customers and offer advice on various cuts of meat.
- Greengrocers sell fruit, vegetables and sometimes flowers. Greengrocers go early to wholesale fruit and vegetable markets to buy stock.
- Delicatessen assistants sell cheese, smallgoods, olives, fish and other specialist items.

EDUCATION AND TRAINING

On-the-job training is often provided for entry level positions. However, specialist knowledge can be obtained by completing TAFE certificates and apprenticeships which will provide an advantage.

SUPERMARKET CHECKOUT OPERATOR

JOB DESCRIPTION

Supermarket checkout operators use cash registers to record and receive payment for goods purchased. They need to be friendly, physically fit and able to stand for long periods of time.

RANGE OF WORK:

- scan barcodes of purchased goods
- operate the till
- weigh fruits and vegetables
- take payments and calculate change
- pack goods in bags or boxes
- answer customer queries
- cash up the till

EDUCATION AND TRAINING

Checkout operators do not need formal qualifications and are usually given in-store training.

FOOD STORE MANAGER

JOB DESCRIPTION

A food store manager supervises the day-to-day running of the store. A manager should have organisational, leadership and team-building skills.

RANGE OF WORK:

- hire and train staff
- organise staff rosters
- order stock
- decide on the layout of the shop
- make security arrangements for the shop
- keep financial records
- keep staff up-to-date with product information

EDUCATION AND TRAINING

Although there are no formal educational requirements, experience in retail or selling is essential when it comes to looking for a job as a manager. Supermarket chains often provide training but it is also possible to complete a traineeship in retail management through a TAFE college.

SALES ASSISTANT

JOB DESCRIPTION

Sales assistants at food stores help to sell food to customers by answering questions and giving advice on products. They need to enjoy dealing with people and should have a friendly, helpful manner. Sales assistants must also be well presented and have good interpersonal skills.

RANGE OF WORK:

- receive stock
- unpack and price goods
- stock shelves
- answer customer queries
- take payment and pack goods in bags
- take orders and arrange deliveries

EDUCATION AND TRAINING

Although many people work as sales assistants without formal qualifications, it is possible to do an apprenticeship in retail operations. Working in some specialist areas, such as butchery, requires an apprenticeship with an employer who can supervise training.

MY STORY

'Work for someone else before you set up your own business"

I studied for a bachelor of education and taught for a few years before changing careers entirely and opening an organic fruit and vegetable shop. There were no local organic produce shops near me and the supermarket's organic section was very limited and over-priced.

Running a business is hard and I've learned a lot since we opened. I like being my own boss and having that sense of control. On the other hand I practically live in the shop, which can restrict my social life.

A few words of advice:
Work for someone else before you set up your own business, then you can learn from their mistakes.

MARC HUDSON
FOOD STORE OWNER

PREPARING AND SERVING FOOD

People who prepare and serve food are part of the hospitality industry. This industry offers a wide range of employment opportunities. The knowledge and skills gained in the industry can be used all over the world.

CHEF

JOB DESCRIPTION

Chefs plan, prepare and cook food in hotels, restaurants, cafés, bars, trains, cruise ships, ferries, airports and canteens. The head chef is in charge of the kitchen and sometimes works with junior and apprentice chefs. Chefs need to be creative, practical, organised and able to work under pressure.

RANGE OF WORK:

- plan and work out the costs of menus
- order food and equipment
- create recipes
- prepare and cook food
- present food attractively
- supervise cleaning and dishwashing
- understand workplace safety and health regulations

EDUCATION AND TRAINING

Although some chefs are self-taught, the more common way for chefs to gain employment is to undertake an apprenticeship where they combine working with studying at a TAFE or a registered training organisation.

KITCHENHAND

JOB DESCRIPTION

Kitchenhands help cooks and chefs in the kitchen. They need to be prepared to follow instructions and to work as part of a team. They also need to be able to work quickly and under pressure.

RANGE OF WORK:

- wash, peel and chop a variety of foods
- prepare salads and desserts
- wash dishes
- dispose of rubbish
- clean kitchen equipment
- collect dirty linen.

EDUCATION AND TRAINING

Most kitchenhands learn what to do on-the-job. There are no formal educational requirements though a diploma or certificate in food preparation can increase employment opportunities.

WAITER

JOB DESCRIPTION

Waiters serve food and drinks to guests in hotels, restaurants and clubs. Waiters need patience and good communication skills. They also need to be highly organised and calm under pressure.

RANGE OF WORK:

- set tables with cutlery, plates and glasses
- greet and show customers to their tables
- explain menus
- take orders and pass them to the kitchen
- serve food and drink
- clear away dishes and clean tables
- make up bills and take payments

EDUCATION AND TRAINING

Waiters do not need any formal educational qualifications or training. Most of the skills they need can be learned on-the-job. Many TAFE colleges offer certificates and short courses in hospitality.

FOOD SERVICE MANAGER

JOB DESCRIPTION

Food service managers organise the supply and preparation of food to people in hospitals, nursing homes, universities and other institutions. They need good communication, organisational and management skills.

RANGE OF WORK:

- plan nutritious and interesting menus
- oversee the purchase and preparation of food
- liaise with dietitians and head chefs
- manage the catering for functions
- supervise and train staff
- monitor standards of service and preparation
- organise rosters and work schedules
- write reports and prepare budgets
- purchase and check equipment

EDUCATION AND TRAINING

There are no formal qualifications required for this job. Experience working in the hospitality industry is usually required, and experience in a similar area could help chances of employment. It would also help to have a diploma or a degree in hospitality or hospitality management.

MY STORY

Whether you call it home economics, food technology or hospitality, my job is to teach people to prepare food. It's a dying art in these days of take-away and pre-packaged food, but people are still keen to learn. I used to work as a chef but I got sick of working in the evening and at weekends so I did a bachelor of education and got a teaching job almost immediately. We don't just teach the practical stuff, we cover nutrition and health as well. I really like my job. The only thing I don't really like is the endless clearing up.

A few words of advice:
Do something else for a couple of years before you start teaching. Perhaps work in hospitality, so you have some experience to bring to the classroom.

HELEN RUSSELL
HOSPITALITY TEACHER

'have some experience to bring to the classroom'

FOOD AND SCIENCE

Food production is becoming more scientific and technical. Genetically modified crops, new ways of processing and improved health and safety standards are just some of the ways that science is improving the way we access foods.

FOOD SCIENTIST

JOB DESCRIPTION

Food scientists analyse food samples to find ways to make foods safer and more nutritious. Food scientists need to be methodical and analytical in their approach. A food scientist's job varies according to their area of research or expertise.

RANGE OF WORK:

- test food for colour, flavour, and nutrition
- find ways of improving the taste, appearance and nutritional value of foods
- research ways of processing, preserving and packaging food
- test to see how food changes when processed
- monitor the quality and safety of food
- help and advise on product development

EDUCATION AND TRAINING

Food scientists need a university degree in science or applied science with a major in food science and technology. Many food scientists have postgraduate qualifications.

DAIRY PROCESSING TECHNICIAN

JOB DESCRIPTION

Dairy processing technicians help to maintain and develop improved methods of milk production, preservation, and food use. They need to be thorough, organised and reliable in their approach.

RANGE OF WORK:

- test milk and milk products to make sure health standards are met
- monitor levels of **microbes**, taste, appearance and nutritional value of milk and milk products
- assist to develop dairy products
- monitor the safe handling, processing, storage and transport of raw materials

EDUCATION AND TRAINING

There are no specific educational requirements for this job, but TAFE qualifications in dairy farming or food health and safety would be advantageous.

AGRICULTURAL SCIENTIST

JOB DESCRIPTION

Agricultural scientists study soils, pastures and crops in order to prevent disease and increase output. They need good observational and analytical skills and should be accurate and objective.

RANGE OF WORK:

- develop animal vaccines to prevent diseases
- find ways of controlling pests and diseases
- research ways of improving farming methods to increase production
- research the effects of farming on the environment
- read, write and present research papers

EDUCATION AND TRAINING

Agricultural scientists must complete a degree in science and major in agriculture or horticulture-related subjects.

ANIMAL SCIENTIST

JOB DESCRIPTION

Animal scientists study farm animals and all aspects of their environment. They need to be observant, accurate, open-minded and logical in the way they think.

RANGE OF WORK:

- research methods of **incubation** and **artificial insemination**
- study genetics and the way animals inherit traits
- crossbreed animals to improve specimen quality
- research parasite and disease control
- study the nutritional requirements of animals and develop feed to meet those requirements
- research and develop improved practices in feeding, housing and sanitation
- study the effects of farming practices

EDUCATION AND TRAINING

Animal scientists need a bachelor of science with a major in zoology, ecology or biology. Many animal scientists have postgraduate qualifications.

MY STORY

'Be flexible about where you want to go'

I moved from Melbourne to Sydney to study for a bachelor of nutrition and dietetics. It usually takes four years but I took a year off in the middle to travel. I wanted to work in hospitals advising on nutrition but was having trouble getting a job. I went to the UK and was offered a job in a hospital in Scotland. Now I'm back in Australia working part-time in a hospital and writing resource material for teachers to use in schools. I can't think of any downsides to working as a dietitian and I love the variety of opportunities this job offers.

A few words of advice:
Be flexible about where you want to go with your skills as there are many different and interesting paths to take.

HAYLEY DEAN
DIETITIAN

GET FUTURE READY

If you think you might be interested in a career in food production, there are a few things that you can do right now that might be useful later. Why not research your education pathways to see what options are available to you. Maybe you could plan the qualification route that you might like to follow, or investigate the practical steps you could take to gain experience in the types of work that interest you.

THE FUTURE

PRACTICAL EXPERIENCE

- learn to grow your own vegetables
- keep chickens and collect the eggs
- learn to bake bread and cakes
- tour a vineyard and find out what is involved
- talk to people in the industry that interests you
- find holiday or weekend work in various areas of food production
- apply for work experience on a farm

DO YOU NEED QUALIFICATIONS?

Many jobs in food production need qualifications. However, there are some jobs that only require enthusiasm and a willingness to learn. Studying for a certificate through a TAFE college usually requires a pass at year 10. Entry to a diploma course requires a pass at year 12. Studying for a university degree usually requires completion of year 12, but sometimes a TAFE qualification can lead to a degree course. Having qualifications will not guarantee you a job, but it can help you gain many of the skills that employers require.

GLOSSARY

apprenticeship way of learning a trade by working with an experienced person while studying
aquaculture cultivation and rearing of water animals and plants
artificial insemination artificial transfer of sperm into a female to create a pregnancy
calving when a cow gives birth to a calf
chocolatier chef who specialises in producing and cooking with chocolate
clarifying removal of impurities by heating, straining and allowing to cool
crutching cutting away of dirty, wet wool around a sheep's tail
cultivate process of growing crops from seeds or plant cuttings and caring for them
cure preservation by salting, smoking or drying
dehydrating drying food to remove moisture for preservation
dipping washing sheep by dipping them in a vermin-killing solution
fermentation process of sugar converting to carbon dioxide and alcohol
fortifying process of strengthening wine with alcohol
freelance self-employed person, offering services for a set amount of time or single project
ganache glaze, icing, sauce or filling made from melting chocolate and cream together
genetically modified when the genetic make-up of an organism is deliberately altered
horticulture science or art of growing fruit, vegetables, flowers and crops
incubation keeping eggs warm so that they will hatch
irrigate process of diverting water through channels to reach crops
livestock farm animals including sheep, cows and horses
mechanised work that is done by a machine
microbes types of bacteria that cause disease
muster rounding up of a herd of animals
orchardists people who grow fruit
parasites organisms that live on other living things and damage them
pâtissiers chef who specialises in making pastries
preserve prepare food in such a way that it will last longer before perishing
pulses edible seeds such as lentils and chick peas
quotas maximum amount of something that is permitted by law
rennet curdled milk containing rennin
retail sale of goods to the public
royal jelly substance produced by bees that is fed to the queen bee or used in beauty products
TAFE Technical And Further Education
traineeship on-the-job training combined with study for a recognised qualification
venison meat from deer
vermin animals that damage or kill crops or farm animals
viticulture cultivation of grapevines for wine or fruit
wholesale selling directly to retailers rather than selling directly to the public

INDEX